Arguing

Deal with it

word by word

Elaine Slavens • Illustrated by Steven Murray

James Lorimer & Company Ltd., Publishers
Toronto

You're yelling at the

top of your lungs, hurling hateful words

at someone who is screaming right back

at you.

How did you end up in such a horrible argument? Or maybe you are one of those people who will do just about anything to avoid getting into an argument. It doesn't matter how unfair the situation is, how nasty someone is acting, or how many times you've been here before — you just want everyone to get along. So you just tell people what they want to hear, and then go off and stew about it.

All people get into disagreements.

That's a fact of life. When you start with different points of view and add a lot of emotion — it's an argument just waiting to happen.

People are always going to disagree about things,

but if you don't learn how to talk it out, that conflict can lead to strained friendships, health problems, stress at school, trouble at home, and — at its worst — real violence.

Whether you have a problem with arguing or are just tired of having arguments erupt around you, this book is for you. You will learn about arguments, what causes them, how to stop them, and how to restore the peace.

Contents

Arguing 101   4
The Challenger   14
The Dodger   20
The Peacemaker   28
More Help   32

We've all been there...

You know, blasting someone or being blasted. But not every disagreement ends up in a shouting match. Arguments are heading for trouble when they involve:

Tears

Someone's feelings getting hurt

Someone taking it personally

Threats

Worrying about it for a long time

Misunderstandings

Physical fighting

Not speaking to each other

Ongoing feuds

Involving other people

Swallowing your anger

Avoiding each other

Getting revenge

Hey, you don't have to agree on everything. But when people are so upset they can't listen to each other's side of things, that's pointless arguing.

Arguing 101

CONTROL

JUSTINE IS GOING TO A PARTY BUT HER MOM DOESN'T LIKE HER OUTFIT...

You're not going out in that.

You're being an old-fashioned witch.

Arguments might *really*

ISSUES

ATTENTION: NEW SCHOOL POLICY

THE NEW SCHOOL POLICY SAYS NO HIP HOP MUSIC IN SCHOOL...

That's stupid.

Why? Hip hop bashes white people.

FRIENDSHIP

JILLIAN AND DARLENE WERE BEST FRIENDS...

WHEN DARLENE GOT A BOYFRIEND, JILLIAN FELT NEGLECTED...

COMPROMISE

mr. PIZZA

GEORGE AND DANNY ARE TRYING TO CHOOSE A PLACE FOR LUNCH...

Let's go to Mr. Pizza, I love their pizza.

We always go there, let's go for Chinese.

↑ 1 BLOCK ↑ WONG'S CHINESE

be about . . .

QUIZ

When you disagree with someone, do you have to win? Do you fold like a deck of cards? Do you keep the peace? Take this quiz and find out which conflict category you fall into below.

1 When you are discussing an important issue, do you:

A. Interrupt people whenever you think of a good point?
B. Have trouble getting your points across?
C. Listen carefully to the other person's side before presenting yours?

2 You are in an argument with someone in your class. Do you:

A. Glare at them threateningly?
B. Smile and pretend you're not upset about how they're talking to you?
C. Stop the argument before it gets out of hand?

3 A casual chat in the lunchroom with your friend has turned into a quarrel. You both have jumped up from your chairs. Do you:

A. Have an "in your face" stance?
B. Have a "don't come near me" stance?
C. Take a deep breath and suggest you both sit down again?

4 Your parents aren't convinced they should extend your curfew. Do you:

A. Lie about how late your friends can stay out?
B. Start crying so they will feel guilty and change their minds?
C. Ask if you can prove yourself with a trial run?

5 In a heated discussion, when the other person is talking, do you:

A. Pretend to listen, but really try to think of snappy responses?
B. Try to listen, but worry that they are getting mad at you?
C. Repeat their points back to them to ensure you understand?

6 You are in a group and a decision has to be made. Do you:

A. Dominate the discussion until they all agree with you?
B. Suggest a decision you think will make the most people happy?
C. Ask everyone for their views before taking a vote?

9 No matter who you disagree with, do you feel:

A. You need to get your way?
B. You need the other person to like you?
C. It's important to hear them out?

7 Your friend has brought up things you've done in the past that have nothing to do with the present argument. Do you:

A. Bring up her past?
B. Get upset about being such a jerk?
C. Ask her to please stick to the issue at hand?

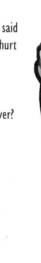

10 Your best friend has said something that really hurt your feelings. Do you:

A. Get him back?
B. Worry the friendship is over?
C. Tell him how you feel?

8 You are in the middle of a dispute, and realize that what your opponent has been saying makes a lot of sense. Do you:

A. Keep hammering away at your point?
B. Start apologizing profusely?
C. Admit you've changed your mind?

If you answered mostly A, you are a **Challenger**. Many Challengers think that all arguments end with one person winning and the other losing.

If you answered mostly B, you are a **Dodger**. Sometimes Dodgers swallow their feelings or opinions and give in because they're afraid of conflict.

If you answered mostly C, you are a **Peacemaker**. A Peacemaker may act like a referee when arguments break out.

Whether you think you are a Challenger, a Dodger or a Peacemaker, read on to learn about ways to resolve disagreements so all sides win.

Dear Conflict Counsellor

Q: Am I too sensitive? I always feel so awful after an argument.   — *Thin-skinned*

A: There is nothing wrong with having a difference of opinion with someone and discussing your views. But we can get very emotional about issues that are important to us, and that's when tempers flare and feelings can get hurt.

Q: I get in a lot of arguments. They turn into physical fights and I get in trouble. How can I stop? — *Big Talker*

A: Congratulations for being willing to make a change! When you feel an argument coming on, take some deep breaths and think about what might happen if things spiral out of control. It'll take practice to cool down, but it gets easier.

Q: What should I do when I don't agree with an adult? — *Intimidated*

A: If you want to be treated with respect, you have to show respect — no matter how old the other person is. And follow these suggestions:
• Once you've calmed down, choose an appropriate place and time to bring up the issue.
• Think carefully about what you want to say.
• Be confident that what you think matters.

Q: Lately my boyfriend and I have been bickering a lot. Is this normal? — *The Bickersons*

A: All relationships have issues that need to be resolved so you can enjoy each other's company. It's important to work together to find solutions that are fair and safe for both of you. If talking openly doesn't work, maybe you can get some helpful strategies from a trusted adult such as a guidance counsellor, teacher, or relative.

Q: My parents are always arguing, and it upsets me a lot. What can I do? — *Uneasy Eavesdropper*

A: Disagreements happen, but it's how your parents work out their problems that is important. If their arguments never get resolved, or turn really ugly or violent, then it's time for them to get counselling. Remember, you know there's a better way, and you don't have to make the same mistakes as your parents or friends.

Myths

Every argument has a winner and a loser.

When both sides understand each other's points of view, everyone wins.

If you have nothing nice to say, don't say anything at all.

You should always try to be polite, but that doesn't mean you have to agree with everyone.

Just turn the other cheek.

If you don't let someone know how you feel, they may continue to treat you disrespectfully.

DID YOU KNOW?

• Anger and other negative feelings | can lead to health problems.

An EYE for an EYE

Getting back at someone can set up an unending cycle of revenge.

Children should be seen and **not heard**.

Young people have every right to express their opinions and should be treated — and treat others — with respect.

She's always got to have

Having the last word doesn't mean the disagreement has been resolved.

the last word.

- High blood pressure, heart problems, obesity, skin disorders, headaches, and stomach problems can result from unresolved arguments.

- Some experts believe that holding in anger during an argument is a primary cause of anxiety.

Why do people always accuse you of picking arguments?

You can't help it if you're always right! So you're a little opinionated, a bit stubborn, and sometimes insensitive. And, okay, occasionally you get kind of loud, but that doesn't make you argumentative — does it?

DEAR DR. SHRINK-WRAPPED...

Q. My sister picks arguments with everyone around her. She says that if she doesn't stick up for herself, nobody else will. But soon no one will want to hang around her. What's her problem?

— *Mystified Sister*

Q. I don't start arguments — I swear! But when I politely pointed out that my friend was wrong, we both got angry and ended up arguing. What can I do now to set things right?

— *After the Fact*

A. Dr. Shrink-Wrapped thinks it's great that you are trying to understand what's going on with your sister. There are many reasons why your sister might start an argument:

*   To get others to do what she wants

*   As a reaction to fear, loss, or disappointment

*   As a reaction to pain, frustration, or annoyance

*   Because she likes being the center of attention, even negative attention

*   Because she enjoys a good debate but doesn't know how to fight fairly

It may be that your sister is just going through an argumentative phase, but let her know that you care and that she can talk to you when she has things to get off her chest. You could also share ways of expressing yourself that don't turn people off.

A. Dr. Shrink-Wrapped says, "It takes two!" You may not think you started the argument, but more often than not, they come about because people need to prove themselves right at any cost.

If you aren't able to avoid the anger and hurt feelings of an argument, take responsibility for your actions. Try to apologize and make things better. Do it privately and remember that it sometimes takes time for people to forgive.

QUIZ

Always arguing?

Who gets things started: you or other people? Take this quiz and see what you can find out. Of the following statements, how many are true, how many false?

1 I try to intimidate other people.

2 When people get upset, I accuse them of being babies.

3 People say I never listen.

4 People lie to win arguments.

5 It's silly for other people to get upset about issues.

6 I raise my voice when having a discussion.

7 Name-calling is okay when you are arguing.

8 People say I'm rude.

9 I use threats when arguing.

10 All's fair in an argument.

11 I sometimes push people around.

12 If people don't agree with me, they're not worth my time.

13 I always have to win an argument.

Swearing is okay when you are arguing. **14**

I'm almost always right. **15**

Once I've made up my mind, I never change it. **16**

People should take my advice. **17**

Most other people are losers. **18**

If a person makes one mistake, they can never be trusted again. **19**

I need people to agree with me. **20**

I never admit I'm wrong. **21**

I have to have the last word. **22**

I never let people forget if they have done something wrong. **23**

Every argument is about who is right and who is wrong. **24**

I hold grudges. **25**

When someone beats me in an argument, I have to even the score. **26**

I am smarter and more informed than most people. **27**

I don't see the point in agreeing to disagree. **28**

It is important for me to get my way. **29**

No issue is too small to get into an argument about. **30**

Did you score a lot of Trues? Maybe it's time to take responsibility for your part in starting arguments and keeping them going. You might want to talk to someone about your need to control other people.

The Challenger

Sometimes we find ourselves squabbling before we even realize what we're doing.

When that happens, a lot of Challengers just dig in their heels and try to win. Here are some sure-fire ways to keep an argument going.

Bulldozing

Argument not going your way? If you try to scare the other person by using aggressive behaviour — verbal or physical — you create more tension. No one likes being pushed around, and you may find yourself with nobody to argue with but yourself.

Old News

Think old incidents and problems you have with your opponent are fair game? Yes, if your game is to take the focus away from the current problem, and to make people angry.

Personal Attack

What about attacking your opponent's personality, views, or values? You will be too busy trying to come up with complaints and insults to listen to the other person's point of view. And fuelling your opponent's anger makes resolving the argument next to impossible.

Being "Above It All"

If you know it's an argument you can't win, do you dismiss the problem as beneath you? Hate to burst your balloon, but everyone sees right through that. If it's an important issue, it is worth your time and effort to try to resolve the argument.

DID YOU KNOW ?

- Unresolved arguments can really hurt relationships if the angry person becomes hostile, sarcastic, critical, or violent.

do's and don'ts

✓ Do try to calm down before you say something that you will regret.

✓ Do try to understand the other person's point of view.

✓ Do try to reach a mutual agreement.

✓ Do try not to offend the other person when you argue.

✓ Do talk to a trusted adult (teacher, counsellor) if you are always getting into arguments with people.

✓ Do think about how your arguing is negatively affecting your relationships with people.

✓ Do praise yourself for the times you do stop yourself from getting into an argument.

✗ Don't resort to physical fighting, even if you are really angry.

✗ Don't intimidate others during an argument in order to get what you want.

✗ Don't take out your anger and frustration on others.

✗ Don't try to always be right.

✗ Don't give up if you slip into old habits of arguing — keep focused on your successes.

✗ Don't feel that you have to argue in order to always prove your point — there are other more effective ways to do this.

✗ Don't think that once you start an argument you have to continue it.

Mountains out of Molehills

Do you have to win every battle, no matter how trivial the issue? If you turn every little conflict into a full-scale war, pretty soon your friends may decide you're not worth all the trouble.

- Holding back anger during an argument can make a person more likely to have an accident.

- Focusing on common needs in an argument is an important step in resolving the problem.

The **Dodger**

You wish they would just leave you alone,

but there they are, in your face.

"Okay, you win," you always say, just to get it over with. People often tell you that you're a great friend, a good listener, nice to have around — and you'd like to keep it that way. But sometimes you think there's such a thing as too nice. Sometimes it makes you mad that the other person, the one picking the argument, gets to feel like they were right and you wind up feeling … bulldozed. But you know what? You don't have to choose between fighting back and giving up. You can resolve disagreements and still avoid a full-blown confrontation like the great friend that you are.

do's and don'ts

✓ Do focus your discussion on a single issue.

✓ Do agree that there is a problem.

✓ Do try to work together to work out the problem.

✓ Do listen carefully to what the other person is saying during an argument. Listening is not necessarily agreeing.

✓ Do brainstorm as many solutions as possible.

✓ Do choose and agree on a solution that is good for both of you.

✓ Do leave the door open for future discussions if this solution doesn't work well.

✓ Do learn how to walk away from an argument if you think it will only lead to trouble.

✓ Do ask for time out if the argument is getting out of hand.

✓ Do get adult help if the argument is not resolved.

✗ Don't lose your cool.

✗ Don't lose focus. Stick to the issue at hand.

✗ Don't interrupt the other person.

✗ Don't be disrespectful.

✗ Don't be afraid to tell how you feel about the issue.

✗ Don't settle for solutions that are unsafe or unfair.

QUIZ

What would you do?

There are lots of ways to deal with someone who is picking an argument with you. Think about how you would respond in each of the following situations. Decide which response would best help you resolve the disagreement without resorting to arguing, and then check your answers on the bottom of page 25.

① PARTY LINE

You accidentally forgot to invite a friend to your party. The next day she tearfully tells you that she is no longer your friend, and calls you insulting names. Do you:

A. Yell insults back at her?
B. Walk away from her, but feel bad afterwards?
C. Let her vent, apologize, then ask her how you can make it up to her?

② BORROWING TROUBLE

You borrowed your brother's favourite CD without him knowing, and then you loaned it to a friend who lost it. Your brother is furious. Do you:

A. Tell him not to be such a baby about it?
B. Offer to give him money to cover the cost of the CD?
C. Tell him that he never takes care of his stuff so it's really his fault anyway?

③ Love Hurts

Your jealous boyfriend has trouble controlling his anger. You tell him you want to break up because it just isn't working and he goes ballistic. Do you:

A. Get into a screaming fight?
B. Get out of there until he cools down enough to talk it out?
C. Run out on him and tell all your friends what a jerk he is.

④ Room Service

Your mom is furious! She asked you to clean your bedroom, but you forgot. Now she won't let you go out until your room is spotless. Do you:

A. Suggest you clean part of your room now, and the rest later?
B. Sneak out of the house later for revenge?
C. Cry and end up with a pounding headache?

⑤ NOT-SO-HOT SHOT

You miss a shot and your teammate yells at you for making the whole team lose the basketball game. Do you:

A. Blame the guy who bumped into you during the game?
B. Shrug and walk away, but feel embarrassed and sick about it later?
C. Tell him you tried your best and will try even harder next time?

Continues . . .

⑥ MAD MAX

You accidentally bump into a guy in your school who has a real rage problem — rumour has it that he blows his top over the smallest thing. Do you:

A. Sock him in the nose before he has a chance to hit you?
B. Run for your life?
C. Apologize immediately and explain that it was an accident?

⑦ Test of Friendship

Your friend blasts you because you didn't give her the answers during a test. She accuses you of not being a real friend. Do you:

A. Offer to help her study for the next test?
B. Accuse her of being a cheater and a whiner?
C. Tell her that you didn't know that she wanted the answers during the test.

8 BIKE STRIFE

Your friend accuses you of breaking his bike when you borrowed it — and it turns out he's right. Do you:

A. Apologize and offer to help fix it?
B. Deny that you broke his bike, and walk away in a huff?
C. Brush him off? He took a chance when he lent it to you.

9 Grief over Grades

Your dad is really mad about your terrible grades. He says you're not allowed to play in your team's upcoming game. Do you:

A. Pretend to listen, then go to the game anyway?
B. Yell, break things, and call him names?
C. Offer to make a study schedule that you will follow if he let's you play in the game?

10 LATE SLIP

Your friend is upset because you are ten minutes late to meet her. She accuses you of always being late just to ruin her plans. Do you:

A. Accuse her of being anal retentive?
B. Apologize, and tell her that you will try to be on time from now on?
C. Let her yell at you and hope she'll calm down eventually.

Answers

1. c   2. b   3. b   4. a   5. c   6. c   7. a   8. a   9. c   10. b

The **Dodger**

There are some basic things you can do when a
disagreement threatens to become an argument.

It is really important to listen to identify the problem. When you have good eye contact and an open posture, you are showing that you understand and accept the messages that are being given.

Encourage
Get other people to state the main ideas in their own words:
"Can you tell me more about…?"
"What else do you know about it?"

Clarify
Ask specific questions to be sure you understand everything:
"When did this happen?"
"Where were you at the time?"

Restate
Once you think you've got the other person's perspective, summarize the problem back:
"So you went to your friend's place at 10?"
"So you didn't want to return the book today?"
"These seem to be the key ideas …"

Reflect
Show you understand how the other person is feeling, and validate their effort to help you understand:
"You seem very upset."
"You look very angry now."
"I can see you really want to resolve this problem."

DID YOU KNOW?

- Brainstorming is a technique used in resolving arguments.

- Some people are professional mediators. Their job is

When Anger Is Involved

Getting angry or upset can turn a disagreement or debate into an argument. If you find that you are having trouble focusing on the issue at hand, count to ten, take some deep breaths, and try to relax. You might ask for a few minutes to calm down — it will give the other person a chance to cool off as well.

You can try self-talk to calm down and refocus:

- "This is going to be okay. I can work this out."
- "Things will get better soon."
- "I don't have to prove myself."
- "I'm not going to let this get to me."
- "I'm not going to take this too seriously."
- "Getting angry is not going to help me resolve this situation."
- "I have what it takes to stay calm in this situation."

Oops! Too late. You blew your stack. Try to turn your angry thoughts into a change for the better by:

- Telling the person you are angry with how you feel.
- Figuring out a plan of action.
- Channelling your angry energy into a physical activity or volunteer work.
- Brainstorming ideas to solve the problem.
- Trying to accept situations that you can't change.

to help two disagreeing people come to a solution.

- Arguments that aren't resolved can destroy friendships.

- Interrupting, offering unwanted advice, preaching, judging, lecturing, insulting, and ridiculing are communication killers.

The **Peacemaker**

You are at school and two of your friends are at each other's throats.

You wish they'd stop it, but there's no way to get involved without picking sides, right?

Well, that depends. Did your friends ask you to get involved? Can you stay neutral? Do you have strong feelings about the issue at hand that will make it hard to not become part of the argument yourself? As a witness, you do have the power to help people who are arguing and need help.

Peer Power

The secret to becoming an effective Peacemaker is to think of conflict as an opportunity — to improve relationships, find solutions, and ensure everyone's needs are met. Some schools have peer mediation programs, special training for students in the skills and strategies of settling conflicts. Once students have completed their training, they act as referees, or "conflict managers," helping other students understand each side of their disagreement to work out their problems together.

Dissolving Disagreements

Problem-solving involves a few basic steps:
- Establish what the problem is.
- Brainstorm for solutions.
- For each solution, determine:
  - if it is safe
  - how people feel about it
  - if it is fair
  - if it will work
- Choose a solution and put it into action.

Remember, not all people appreciate someone helping them with their arguments, and you have to respect their wishes. You may be able to help after the disagreement by listening carefully to the person who wants your help and suggesting some strategies.

do's and don'ts

✓ Do set a good example for others. Treat others respectfully and fairly.

✓ Do try to help people calm down if they are very upset about an argument.

✓ Do respect people's wishes if they prefer to work it out on their own without your help.

✓ Do be an attentive and empathetic listener if a friend or family member wants to talk to you about a problem.

✓ Do try to come up with lots of possible solutions, then help them choose the best one.

✓ Do offer your support to a friend or relative who needs your help.

✓ Do talk to someone if someone else's argument has upset you.

✓ Do try to identify the problem and the feeling behind it.

✗ Don't force your ideas on people when they are upset about an argument. What people usually need is an empathetic listener.

✗ Don't break someone's trust by spreading information about the argument. That could easily start another argument — this time with you!

✗ Don't get sucked into taking sides in an argument.

The **Peacemaker**

QUIZ

To get involved or not?

No one can tell you the right thing to do when you are witness to an argument. The important thing to remember is that you have choices. What would you do in the following situations? This quiz has no right or wrong answers, because each argument is unique. Your answers may be different from the suggestions, but they could be right under the circumstances.

Money Woes

1 Your best friend calls you and says she keeps locking horns with her mom about her allowance. What should you do?

- Listen carefully to her story.
- Suggest to her some strategies for calming down.
- Ask questions about the details.
- Ask her what she thinks the problem is.
- Brainstorm some possible solutions to the problem.
- Give her some suggestions on how to approach her mom to discuss the issue.

Bad Boyfriend

2 Your best friend is in tears. She confides in you that her boyfriend calls her horrible, degrading names when they quarrel.

- Ask her what her thoughts are about the situation and listen carefully.
- Discuss the possibility of her telling him very clearly how she is feeling.
- Tell her you are there for her and doesn't need to stay with someone who makes her feel bad about herself.

Bickering Brothers

3 Your younger brothers are always bickering about who gets to watch the TV. They come to you for help.

- Tell them how proud you are of them for wanting to work out the problem together.
- Listen to each brother's side of the problem.
- Have them suggest a list of possible solutions. You can also help with this.
- Have them agree on one of the solutions.
- Tell them to try it, and meet back in a few days to see how it's working.

30

Adult Arguing

9 You see two adults on the street having a really horrible argument, and they are beginning to push each other around. It looks as though they are going to get into a serious physical fight.

- Tell another adult who is nearby.
- If the argument escalates into a fight, dial 911 on your cell phone or the nearest pay phone.
- Take note of what these men look like in case the police officer asks you later, but keep your distance.

FURIOUS FRIENDS

5 You overheard two of your friends having a serious discussion that is turning into a argument.

- You ask them what's up, with the hope that this will break the tension.
- You use humour to distract them.
- If they want you to mediate, ask them what the issue is and listen carefully to each person's perspective.
- Have them think up possible compromises and remind them that they can agree to disagree.

- 10% of communication is verbal. The other 90% is non-verbal.
- Many schools have peer mediation programs in which students help other kids resolve their arguments.
- When dealing with an angry person, it's best to stay safe!

More **Help**

It takes time and practice to learn the skills in this book. There are many ways to deal with arguing, but only <u>you</u> can know which is best for each situation. In the end, the best strategy is the one that resolves problems in a respectful and caring way.

If you need more information or someone to talk to, the following Canadian resources may be of help:

Helplines and Organizations

Kids Help Phone (Canada)   1-800-668-6868
Youth Crisis Hotline (USA)   1-800-448-4663

Web sites

Kidshealth.org
Kids Help Phone: www.kidshelp.sympatico.ca
Teenadvice.about.com
Iwannaknow.org

Books

Brothers on Ice by John Danakas. James Lorimer & Company, 2001.
Frog Face and the Three Boys by Don Trembath. Orca Book Publishers, 2000.
Offside! by Sandra Diersch. James Lorimer & Company, 2000.
Out of Bounds by Sylvia Gunnery. James Lorimer & Company, 2004.
Off the Wall by Camilla Reghelini Rivers. James Lorimer & Company, 2001.
Play On by Sandra Diersch. James Lorimer & Company, 2004.
The Reunion by Jacqueline Pearce. Orca Book Publishers, 2002.
Soccer Star! by Jacquie Guest. James Lorimer & Company, 2003.
There you Are by Joanne Taylor. Tundra Books, 2004.
Two False Moves by Ted Staunton. Red Deer Press, 2000.
Worm Pie by Beverly Scudamore. Scholastic Canada, 1997.
Digging for Philip by Greg Jackson-Davis. Great Plains, 2003.

Other titles in the Deal With It series:

Bullying: Deal with it before push comes to shove by Elaine Slavens, illustrated by Brooke Kerrigan.
Competition: Deal with it from start to finish by Mireille Messier, illustrated by Steven Murray.
Fighting: Deal with it without coming to blows by Elaine Slavens, illustrated by Steven Murray.
Gossip: Deal with it before word gets around by Catherine Rondina, illustrated by Dan Workman.
Peer Pressure: Deal with it without losing your cool by Elaine Slavens, illustrated by Ben Shannon.
Racism: Deal with it before it gets under your skin by Anne Marie Aikins, illustrated by Steven Murray.

James Lorimer & Company Ltd. acknowledges the support of the Ontario Arts Council. We acknowledge the support of the Government of Canada through the Book Publishing Industry Development Program (BPIDP) for our publishing activities. We acknowledge the support of the Canada Council for the Arts for our publishing program. We acknowledge the support of the Government of Ontario through the Ontario Media Development Corporation's Ontario Book Initiative.

The Canada Council   Le Conseil des Arts
for the Arts   du Canada

ONTARIO ARTS COUNCIL
CONSEIL DES ARTS DE L'ONTARIO

Design: Blair Kerrigan/Glyphics

Library and Archives Canada Cataloguing in Publication

Slavens, Elaine
      Arguing : deal with it word by word / Elaine Slavens ; illustrated by Steven Murray.

(Deal with it)
Includes bibliographical references.
ISBN 1-55028-820-2

      1. Interpersonal conflict—Juvenile literature.
2. Quarreling—Juvenile literature. 3. Conflict management—Juvenile literature.
I. Murray, Steven II. Title. III. Series: Deal with it (Toronto, Ont.)

BF723.I645S52 2004   j303.6'9   C2004-904308-0

James Lorimer & Company Ltd., Publishers
35 Britain Street
Toronto, Ontario
M5A 1R7
www. lorimer.ca

Distributed in the United States by:
Orca Book Publishers
P.O. Box 468 Custer, WA
USA 98240-0468

Printed and bound in Canada